Lucy Hunt

**Hand-book of light gymnastics**

Lucy Hunt

**Hand-book of light gymnastics**

ISBN/EAN: 9783337269074

Printed in Europe, USA, Canada, Australia, Japan

Cover: Foto ©Lupo / pixelio.de

More available books at **www.hansebooks.com**

# STATE NORMAL SCHOOL,
## LOS ANGELES — CAL.

# HAND-BOOK

OF

# LIGHT GYMNASTICS

By LUCY B. HUNT

LATE INSTRUCTOR IN GYMNASTICS AT SMITH COLLEGE
NORTHAMPTON MASS.

NEW EDITION

BOSTON
LEE AND SHEPARD PUBLISHERS
NEW YORK CHARLES T. DILLINGHAM
1890

# CONTENTS.

|  | PAGE |
|---|---|
| Introduction | 7 |
| Free Gymnastics | 11 |
| Wand Exercises | 21 |
| Ring Exercises | 27 |
| Dumb-Bells | 35 |
| Percussion | 46 |
| Mutual Help Exercises | 49 |
| Bean-Bags | 52 |
| Marching | 54 |
| Chapter on Dress | 80 |
| Gymnastic Music | 88 |

# PREFACE.

IN the preparation of this little handbook of light Gymnastics, I have had in view the often-expressed want of many; which want, so far as I can learn, no one has yet attempted to supply. It is not intended to compete with, or take the place of, the many valuable works on this subject by Dr. Dio Lewis and others; but to give, in an inexpensive form, a condensed yet clear description of the various exercises.

Most books that have been thus far published, are, by reason of illustrations and the additional subjects treated, both expensive and bulky.

Taking the Dio Lewis system as a foundation, I have, during the experience of many years' teaching, added to, taken from, and altered various exercises, resulting in the order now published for the first time in these pages.

I claim, therefore, originality in the arrangement, and in a greater part of the marching figures.

While this book is intended and prepared for the use of my own pupils, and for teachers in colleges and seminaries, it is hoped that it will prove a convenient guide to those who wish to carry on these exercises at home.

# INTRODUCTION.

The exercises here given having been carefully selected, and thoroughly tested, can be practised by any person in ordinary health without injury, if the following conditions are observed:

Never over-work, particularly at the beginning, and avoid all exposure and draughts while resting between and after the exercises.

Go into the gymnasium regularly, without omitting a day, and always in a dress that is correct in every particular.

Attention is called to the carefully prepared chapter on the gymnastic suit.

In all these exercises, the movements are to be performed steadily and gradually, and never with a sudden jerk. Beginning with care and using but little force, increase in vigor from day to day, till all the changes are marked with that precision and dash so essential to their perfect performance.

All movements of the head and body must be slow compared with those of the limbs. What are called free gymnastics, being performed without apparatus of any sort, I place as the simplest form of exercise at the beginning of the list.

The wands come next, and are much easier than the rings and dumb-bells, always provided that the wand is of the requisite length, viz.: just reaching to the armpit when placed on the floor at one's side. The rings are, in my estimation more open to objection than any other exercise, owing to the almost unavoidable inequalities in strength, and length of arm-reach, of those taking part. Great care should be shown in selecting partners, and teachers should insist that they be about equal in height, and general strength. Then there can be no possible danger in these exercises which, in some respects, are the most beautiful of all forms of gymnastic work. The Quartette exercises, when rendered with precision and in perfect unison with the music, are particularly effective. The dumb-bells, with the anvil chorus, must always be taken very slowly. The list of club exercises I shall omit from this book. While they are, for obvious reasons, very valuable, they are more difficult than many others as bringing into play for a longer time unused muscles; and they are also extremely difficult to describe without the aid of illustrations.

# FREE GYMNASTICS.

Position: stand with heels together, hips and shoulders back, hands firmly closed and well back upon the chest.

## First Series.

Each number fills a strain of music except when otherwise specified.

No. 1. Thrust right hand down twice, left twice, alternately twice, together twice.

No. 2. Repeat No. 1, only thrust hands out at sides instead of down.

No. 3. Repeat No. 1, thrusting hands directly up.

No. 4. Repeat No. 1, thrusting hands from shoulders directly forward.

No. 5. Right hand down once, left once,

drum beat (the right hand a little in advance of left) once, together once, half a strain.

No. 6. Same exercise, thrusting out at sides instead of down.

No. 7. Same exercise, only thrusting directly up.

No. 8. Same exercise, only thrusting directly forward from shoulder.

No. 9. Right hand down once, left once, then clap hands through rest of the strain.

No. 10. Same exercise, out at sides.

No. 11. Same exercise, directly up.

No. 12. Same exercise, out in front.

No. 13. Hands on the hips, step with right foot forward, then diagonally forward, directly at side, diagonally back, directly back, cross back of left, cross again still farther back; lastly cross in front of left foot, returning to position after each step.

No. 14. Repeat No. 13, with left foot.

No. 15. Stamp with right foot forward three times, advancing each time, then left three times. Stamp three times back with right foot, same with left.

## Free Gymnastics.

No. 16. Repeat No. 15.

No. 17. Hands still on hips twist body alternately to right and left, twice each ; four beats of music.

No. 18. Bend body alternately to right and left, four beats of music finishing the strain.

No. 19. Bend body alternately forward and back, twice each.

✓ No. 20. Bend body first right, then back, left, front ; reverse, left, back, right, front, finishing the strain.

No. 21. Same as No. 17, only twist the head.

No. 22. Same as No. 18, only bend the head instead of the body.

No. 23. Same as No. 19, with head only.

✓ No. 24. Like No. 20, bend head instead of body, right back, left, front, then reverse.

No. 25. Arms extended in front, bring them forcibly back to chest eight times.

No. 26. Arms again extended, raise right hand twice without bending the elbow, then left twice, alternately twice, together twice.

No. 27. Hands closed on chest, thrust down, out, up, and in front, twisting the arms each thrust; repeat.

No. 28. Thrust hands from chest toward floor without bending the knees. stop on chest, then over head, rising on toes, and opening hands at each thrust, continue in half time through strain.

No. 29. Cross left foot over right, at same time touching fingers over head; then right foot over left, alternately in half time through the strain.

No. 30. Stamp left foot, then right, charge diagonally forward with right foot, bend and straighten right knee, at the same time carrying arms back from horizontal in front. When the arms are extended in front, the hands should be the width of the shoulders apart.

No. 31. Repeat this exercise on the left side.

## Second Series.

Position same as before.

No. 1. Thrust right hand from chest down, then up, twice, same with left hand.

Free Gymnastics. 15

No. 2. Same alternately, right hand going down first as left goes up. Both down, then up twice each.

No. 3. Thrust right hand out at right side, then cross to left alternately through the strain, twisting the body when turning to left.

No. 4. Thrust left hand out at left side, then cross to right, twisting body at right.

No. 5. Thrust both hands to right and left level with shoulders, alternately through the strain, twisting body each time, but keeping feet still.

No. 6. Thrust both hands out at right side four times, then to left four times.

No. 7. Thrust right foot forward and down three times, stamping floor on fourth beat, same with left foot. Thrust right foot back three times, then left, stamping on fourth beat each time. Two strains of music.

No. 8. Hands down at sides, raise right arm over head without bending elbow, twice, then left twice, alternately, then together twice.

No. 9. Arms down at sides, raise right to the side of head twice, then left twice, alternately twice, then together twice.

No. 10. Arms extended in front, swing them back horizontally eight times.

No. 11. Hands down at sides, raise right shoulder twice, left twice, alternately twice, together twice.

No. 12. Hands down at sides, open and shut the fingers four times, out at sides four times.

No. 13. Same over head, same with arms extended in front.

No. 14. Mowing movement with both arms from right to left then from left to right, bending the body forward from the hips.

No. 15. Hands on hips, thrust elbows back eight times.

No. 16. Bend body to right, thrust the hands forward and downward, alternately, four times; the same on the left side.

No. 17. Repeat No. 16.

No. 18. Swing arms around, hitting chest

## Free Gymnastics.

(as teamsters warm their hands), right hand above and then left, eight times.

No. 19. Hands on hips, stamp left foot, then right, step diagonally forward with right foot, sway back and forth, bending right and left knees alternately.

No. 20. Repeat No. 19 on left side.

No. 21. Repeat No. 19, stepping back instead of forward with right foot.

No. 22. Repeat No 21, with left foot.

### Third Series.

Position: heels together, hands on hips.

No. 1. Stamp seven times quickly with right, once slowly with left, once with right, then step diagonally forward with right foot, shoulders back, fill the lungs, then percuss the chest through the rest of the strain.

No. 2. Repeat on left side.

No. 3. Repeat, stepping back with right foot on right side.

No. 4. Repeat, stepping back on left.

No. 5. Clasp hands behind the back, raise and thrust down with force eight times.

No. 6. Hands down at sides, twist them four times half round, same out at sides.

No. 7. Repeat over head, repeat with arms extended in front.

No. 8. Arms extended in front, palms together, without bending the elbows, slide right and left hands alternately through the strain.

No. 9. Hands closed firmly under the armpits, thrust right hand down twice, left twice, alternately twice, together twice.

No. 10. Hands upon shoulders, repeat No. 9, only thrusting up instead of down.

No. 11. Right hand down from armpit, left hand up from shoulder, alternate through four beats.

No. 12. Thrust hands down from armpits, and up from shoulders alternately through the strain.

No. 13. Hands down at sides, carry right arm twice to the horizontal position in front, stopping suddenly with arm on a line with shoulder, left arm twice, alternately twice, together twice.

No. 14. Carry the arms to the perpendicular, and then move them with the whole body from side to side, keeping elbows stiff through the strain.

No. 15. Thrust right down, left out, right out, left up, right up, left out in front, right out in front, left down.

No. 16. Repeat No. 14.

### Chorus.

Music, "Yankee Doodle." always.

Position, heels together, hands closed on chest.

No. 1. Repeat No. 1 of first series.

No. 2. Clap hands through the strain.

No. 3. Percuss chest through the strain.

No. 4. Hop on right foot four times. then on left four times.

No. 5. Repeat No. 2, first series.

No. 6. Clap hands through strain.

No. 7. Percuss the chest.

No. 8. Hop on right and left feet alternately four beats, together four beats.

No. 9. Repeat No. 3, first series.
No. 10. Clap the hands.
No. 11. Percuss the chest.
No. 12. Take long skipping steps, right then left foot alternately through the measure.
No. 13, Repeat No. 4, first series.
No. 14. Clap the hands.
No. 15. Percuss the chest.
No. 16. Take twisted step, one foot crossing the other through the strain.

### Cautions.

Keep the heels together and hips back, unless the exercise otherwise directs. The arms overhead should always be with elbows unbent. Inhale before percussion.

These exercises should be taken slowly and with caution at first. As the strength increases, greater rapidity and force should be employed.

Music for the free gymnastics must always be either in galop or polka time. The polka is better for the first series when taken alone; the galop for the others.

# WAND EXERCISES.

POSITION: heels together, hips and shoulders well back. The wand is held in front of the right shoulder, till first signal from the piano, which consists of three chords struck with both hands, the first being the length of the other two; then drop it horizontally in front of the body. At second signal raise the wand till the arms are extended in horizontal position in front of body, place the hands so as to divide the wand into three equal parts. At third signal, carry the wand back to second position down in front.

No. 1. Raise the wand to chin four times, keeping elbows high, last time carry it abov the head, then bring down under chin four times.

No. 2. Carry wand from above the head

nearly to floor, four times, without bending knees or elbows, then down back of the neck four times.

No. 3. Carry wand from above the head to chin, and then back of neck, alternately four times each.

No. 4. Wand over head. On first beat, carry right hand to right end of wand, on second beat, left hand to left end, then carry hand back of head to hips, six times, keeping elbows stiff.

No. 5. Carry wand back from above head down nearly to floor; and then back to hips, four times, alternately four times each.

No. 6. Carry wand from above the head to right and left sides alternately eight times, keeping elbows stiff and stopping exactly over head each time.

No. 7. On first beat, let go wand with left hand, place end of wand on floor between feet. On second beat place wand on floor at arms length, diagonally forward on right side. Step with right foot to wand through rest of strain, keeping right arm, left knee and wand perfectly straight.

No. 8. Repeat No. 7 on left side.

No. 9. Repeat No. 7, keeping the foot stationary, the knee bending with each accented beat.

No. 10. Repeat No. 9 on left side.

No. 11. Arms horizontal in front, wand held perpendicularly, bring wand back to chest eight times keeping elbows high.

No. 12. Wand and arms in same position, bring wand to right and left shoulders alternately, four times each. In passing the wand from one side to the other, raise the arms straight to a horizontal position in front.

No. 13. Hands in front of chest, point wand diagonally forward at an angle of forty-five degrees, first to the right, then to the left alternately through strain, making the change of hands just in front of chin.

No. 14. With wand pointing in the same direction as in last exercise, step diagonally forward with right and left foot alternately through strain.

No. 15. Repeat No. 14, only step back instead of forward, leading with left foot instead of right, keeping wand pointing forward.

No. 16. Wand horizontal over head, right hand in front, reverse position, bringing left hand in front, on half time through strain.

No. 17. Same position, right face, bend forward bringing wand to perpendicular on right side, four times.

No. 18. Repeat No. 17 on left side.

No. 19. Same movement from side to side changing wand over head.

No. 20. On first beat, put left end of wand on floor in front of feet; on second beat, carry wand at arm's length in front, charge right foot to wand twice, left four times, changing hands and feet at same time.

No. 21. Right foot back four times, right hand on wand, same with left hand and foot.

No. 22. Right foot forward and back four times, left the same, holding wand in same position as last exercise

No. 23. Both hands on wand in front, right foot forward, left back at the same time, reverse and repeat.

No. 24. Front face, place the wand perpendicularly in front of right shoulder, left hand up, carry to front of left, with right hand up eight times. Then carry the wand from front to back of right, then from back of right to back of left eight times. On the fourth time carry from back of right to front of right four times.

No. 25. Wand in front of right shoulder, carry to front of left, then back of left, back of right, front of right. repeat, then reverse.

No. 26. Wand in front of right shoulder, carry to back of left four times, then front of left to back of right four times.

No. 27. Right face, left end of wand on floor, charge right foot to right side, then back, cross back of left foot, then in front of left, repeat with left foot.

No. 28. Repeat No. 27, using right and left foot alternately.

No. 29. Front face, place wand in front of chest, right hand down, left down alternately eight times. Repeat the exercise with wand carried down behind the back.

No. 30. Step diagonally forward, wand behind the back, right end of it up at an angle of forty-five degrees; then step left foot forward, left end of wand up.

No. 31. Place wand horizontally in front, on first beat carry to perpendicular on right side, then to left through the strain.

No. 32. Carry wand horizontally over head, down in front, and charge with wand same as 31, only charge through strain with right and left foot alternately through the strain.

### Caution.

Always select a wand just long enough to reach the armpit when placed on the floor at one's side. All exercises from behind the head or back should be taken with caution, and avoided altogether by those with weak backs.

### Music.

Schottische time is the best, but slow marches and quicksteps can be used.

# RING EXERCISES.

These exercises are performed in couples; partners facing each other about three feet apart; the one standing on right of teacher on platform, holding both rings.

## First Series.

No. 1. On first beat of the music, the ring in right hand is extended, and grasped by partner's right hand, Second beat, right feet together, toes touching, on third beat left feet back at right angles with right feet, with left hands upon the hips. Turn the ring over half way and then back to place through rest of strain, keeping perfect time.

No. 2. Repeat No. 1, only use left hand and left foot instead of right.

No. 3. Repeat No. 1, only first join both hands, on second beat right feet together, third beat step back as before, turn rings through strain.

No. 4. Repeat No. 3, with both hands joined and left feet touching, right feet back, turn rings through strain.

No. 5. On first beat, turn back to back, on second beat left feet together, charge directly forward with right feet: head and shoulders well thrown back pull evenly with partner, and turn the rings through strain.

No. 6. Repeat No. 5 with right feet together, left out in front, turn rings through strain.

No. 7. On first beat, turn face to face, on second beat raise arms above head, then lower rings without bending knees, looking alternately to right and left of partner through strain.

No. 8. First beat, lift arms towards platform, high up at side, the others low down at the opposite side, carry them alternately up and down through half the strain, then both together, half a strain.

No. 9. First beat, turn back to back, second beat, face up and down the hall, hands at once on shoulders thrust up, out and down. twice each.

No. 10. Same position, thrust up, out and down. once each, then repeat till strain ends.

No. 11. First beat, step back to position, second beat, turn face to face, third beat, put left foot inside partner's left, left knee pressed against partner's left, fourth beat, right foot back, long step at right angles with left. Your own right hand and ring against your right shoulder, left hand against partner's right. Thrust with vigor from shoulder to shoulder through strain.

No. 12. Repeat No. 11. with right feet together instead of left, position of hands reversed.

No. 13. First beat. turn back to back, charge diagonally forward with right and left feet alternately through strain.

No. 14. First beat, turn face to face, place left foot inside partner's left, short step back with right foot at right angles with the left. Rings over head held firmly, arms perfectly straight, sway alternately through the strain.

No. 15. Repeat No. 14, with right feet together instead of left.

No. 16. First beat, turn back to back, charge up and down the hall alternately twice each; charge with right feet at same time, then left feet at same time, alternately through rest of strain.

No. 17. First beat, turn face to face, repeat No. 16.

No. 18. First beat, turn back to back, raise outside, then inside arms alternately, then charge on fifth beat directly forward; raise both hands rest of strain.

No. 19. First beat, face up and down the hall, second beat, turn face to face, third beat, spring apart, right feet pointing toward each other, left feet back a short step at right angles with the right feet. Right hands grasping rings, charge with right feet to right of partner, stopping each time suddenly when back to position.

No. 20. Repeat No. 19, using right foot for left, right hand for left.

No. 21. Repeat No. 19, holding rings in both hands, and charging right and left alternately, right foot to left side, left foot to right side.

No. 22. First beat, approach partner, second beat, turn back to back, third beat, face across the hall, place left feet together, fourth beat, step out with right foot, touching shoulders, sway through the strain.

No. 23. Repeat No. 22, using right for left, and left for right.

No. 24. First beat, turn face to face, second beat, face up and down the hall, swing up outside and inside arms alternately: turn face and body each time. This is called the mirror.

No. 25. First beat, turn back to back, swing over outside and inside arms alternately twice, each; then together twice.

No. 26. First beat, turn face to face, with outside arms, second beat, back to back, with outside arms, repeat with inside arms.

No. 27. First beat, face across the hall, turn back to back; second beat, left feet together, third beat, swing hands over head and step forward with right foot, bend and straighten right knees.

No. 28. Repeat No. 27, with right feet together instead of left.

No. 29. First beat, turn face to face, step alternately right feet diagonally forward to left of partner, and left feet to right of partner through strain.

## Quartette Exercises.

Position: four stand together, facing each other, and at arm's length. Each holds a ring in her right hand.

No. 1. First beat, join hands, second beat, step to the centre with right and left feet, alternately raising hands high through strain.

No. 2. First beat, all step to the centre,

## Ring Exercises.

lifting the hands high. step back with right and left feet alternately through strain, carrying rings down.

No. 3. Arms lifted and held firmly, skip through strain, all keeping perfect time and leading with right feet.

No. 4. Outside couple, or couple farthest from platform, pass under the raised arms of the other couple ; and on third beat, rings on shoulders, all thrust at same time, hands up through the strain.

No. 5. The four standing facing ends of hall charge up and down the hall, lifting rings, the others charge directly at the side lifting rings, all charge together diagonally forward, first with right then with left foot, then repeat the whole.

No. 6. Lift hands towards ends of hall, then lift hands towards sides of hall. Lift all the hands twice. Repeat the whole.

No. 7. Stamp first with right foot, then with left, charge diagonally forward with right foot, hands held high over head, sway during strain. Repeat stamping first with left foot.

## Caution.

In all exercises, turning back to back, be careful and not pull suddenly, and never let go the ring before the word is given.

Always stand at such a distance from next couple that there can be no hitting of rings.

The rings should always be strongly made, and about six inches in diameter.

## Music.

The simplest of Strauss's waltzes must be used, or those of other composers similar in style.

# DUMB-BELLS.

Position: Heels together, hips and shoulders back, bells down at sides. One-half of each strain of music is given to the exercise, the other half to what is called "the attitude." In taking these attitudes the bells are brought first to the chest; then, unless otherwise specified, placed upon the hips.

No. 1. Hands down at sides, palms in front, turn bells four times, bringing them to chest on fourth accented beat.

*Attitude:* Step diagonally forward with right foot, carrying hands to hips, looking over right shoulder.

No. 2. Elbows at sides, turn bells just half-way round four times.

*Attitude:* Step diagonally forward with left foot, looking over left shoulder.

No. 3. Arms extended at sides, turn bells four times.

*Attitude:* Step diagonally back with right foot, looking over right shoulder.

No. 4. Arms extended over head, palms in front, turn bells four times.

*Attitude:* Step diagonally back with left foot, looking over left shoulder.

No. 5. Bells far back on chest, thrust both down, out at sides, up, and out in front.

*Attitude:* Turn to the right, throw arms up at side without bending the knees. The bells in this attitude should be exactly horizontal and parallel.

No. 6. Repeat No. 5, turning to the left and throwing the arms up on left side.

*Attitude:* Repeat attitude No. 5.

No. 7. Drop bells at sides, right hand up to armpit once, left once, together twice.

*Attitude:* Drop to sitting position, bells touching the floor, rest through the remainder of the strain.

No. 8. Bells on shoulders, thrust each up once, both together twice.

*Attitude:* Rise on toes, palms forward, bells parallel.

No. 9. Arms extended in front, turn four times.

*Attitude:* Step diagonally forward with right foot, right hand on hip, looking back at left bell, which is extended in left hand.

No. 10. Arms extended sideways at an angle of forty-five degrees, turn bells four times.

*Attitude:* Step forward with left foot, left hand on hip, looking back at right bell, which is extended in right hand.

No. 11. Bells on chest, right hand down, then up, left hand the same.

*Attitude:* Turn body to right, thrust right hand obliquely up, palm up; left hand obliquely down, palm down.

No. 12. Bells on chest, right hand up, left down; reverse, then both down, both up.

*Attitude:* Turn to left, thrust hands up and down as in No. 11.

No. 13. Arms extended in front, palms opposite, right hand up once, left the same, both together up twice.

This should be done without bending the elbows.

*Attitude:* Step diagonally forward with right foot, the body and head thrown forward, and arms thrown wide apart.

No. 14. Repeat No. 13.

*Attitude:* Repeat attitude No. 13 on the left side.

No. 15. Arms extended at sides, right arm up once, left once, both twice, without bending the knees.

*Attitude:* Step diagonally back with right foot, right hand up, with bell perpendicular, left hand on hip.

No. 16. Repeat No. 15.

*Attitude:* Repeat attitude on left side.

No. 17. Arms extended, with bells parallel in front, bring the bells back forcibly upon the chest four times.

*Attitude:* Fold the arms with bells closely pressed against the chest, and bend back slowly from the waist.

## Second Series.

In this series the attitudes precede the exercises.

Position: Same as in the first exercise, with bells down at sides.

*Attitude* No. 1. Stamp left foot, then right, step out at right side with right foot, right arm obliquely up, left arm obliquely down, both palms down, sway. Repeat on left side, four beats on each side.

*Exercise.* Bells down at sides, swing right bell up to perpendicular over head twice, left bell twice, alternately twice, both together twice.

No. 2. Stamp as before, first left foot then right; step to right, with right arm lifted a little above the shoulder, the bell perpendicular, left on shoulder. Repeat on left side.

*Exercise.* Bells down at sides, swing right bell sideways up to perpendicular over head twice, left bell twice, alternately twice.

No. 3. Stamp left foot, then right, step with right foot to right side, carry both bells over head, sway twice. Repeat on left side.

*Exercise.* Hands down in front of knees, with fingers clasping bells together, describe circle over head from right to left and from left to right, alternately, separate hands over head on last beat.

No. 4. Stamp left foot, then right, long diagonal charge, as it is called, on the right side, bells thrust forward from shoulders, twice through half strain of music. Repeat on left side.

*Exercise.* Elbows high, and bells under the chin. Thrust elbows back through whole of strain.

No. 5. Stamp left foot, then right, take short step diagonally forward with right foot, thrust bells up, then down, stopping on line with shoulders, then nearly to the floor. Repeat on left side.

*Exercise.* Horizontal sweep with arms, carrying bells from just in front to side, stopping on line with shoulders.

No. 6. Short diagonal charge, stepping out on right side, thrusting bells up and back twice from the shoulders. Repeat on left side.

*Exercise.* Thrust both bells up on right side, then on left, without moving the feet through whole of the strain.

No. 7. Short diagonal charge, stepping back on right side, thrust bells up twice from shoulders. Repeat on left side.

*Exercise.* Bells on chest, thrust left hand forward, then right, alternately through the strain.

No. 8. Long side charge, stamp left, then right, step directly to right, with right bell on hip, left down at side, swing left up to side of head on fifth beat, turning the hand over on its way up to position. Repeat on left side.

*Exercise.* Right hand following left in the order of No. 14, third series Free Gymnastics.

No. 9. Stamp three times with left foot, stepping diagonally forward with each stamp, looking back at the same time, twisting the right bell, with right arm thrust up and back. Repeat on left side.

*Exercise.* Step diagonally forward with right and left feet alternately, arms extended, as in last attitude, then step at right side, and left arms extended obliquely as in No. 1, two beats. Repeat the step with arms as in No. 3, two beats.

No. 10. Bells on shoulders, thrust right out, palm up, twice, left twice, alternately twice, both together twice.

*Exercise.* Bring bells from shoulders to chest, thrust directly forward, raise over head, back to first position, then nearly touch the floor. Repeat the whole.

No. 11. This is called French, or small-sword exercise: Stamp left foot, then right, then mark time two beats with right foot, stamp twice out at side with same, right arm extended, left arm curved over the head, bell down.

No. 12. Repeat on left side.

### Anvil Chorus.

First position: Left arm extended in front, right bell back of head on shoulder.

No. 1. Strike left bell down with the right, exactly reversing their positions, repeat

## Dumb-Bells. 43

the movement with left bell, swing right bell, striking left bell from under, instead of over. This occupies four beats.

No. 2. Step diagonally forward with right and left feet alternately, striking bells over head.

No. 3. Repeat No. 1.

No. 4. Repeat No. 2, only stepping diagonally backward instead of forward, alternately through the strain.

No. 5. Repeat No. 1.

No. 6. Swing bells to the front with arms extended, strike once in front, once back of the body, once over head; repeat, then strike once over head, and once more behind the back. Bring bells back to first position.

No. 7. Repeat No. 1.

No. 8. Arms extended, strike bells first on one end, then on the other alternately through the strain, lifting the bells slowly with each stroke until on the last they are on a level with the eyes.

No. 9. Repeat No. 1.

No. 10. Step out directly at right side, bending right and left knees alternately. While swaying thus, strike left bell on right which is extended in the right hand.

No. 11.  Repeat No. 1.
No. 12.  Repeat No. 10, on left side.
No. 13.  Repeat No. 1.
No. 14.  Take a short step diagonally forward with the right foot, place the left bell on right knee, and while swaying as in No. 10, strike bell on knee with right bell, carrying the latter in a complete circle.
No. 15.  Repeat No. 1.
No. 16.  Repeat No. 14 on left side.

### Double Anvil Chorus.

Stand in two lines facing partner, take Exercise No. 1, striking partner's bell each time; then charge with right foot each, through the strain, anvil part of No. 1, again charge on the left, anvil part, striking bell on partner's left knee, again the one on right knee; anvil part again. Now strike partner's bell extended in her left hand; repeat on bell of left hand neighbor's bell, extended in her right hand. Repeat last exercise of single anvil chorus.

### Caution.

Step carefully but quickly to all the attitudes.

Rest oftener than in the other exercises.

Use too light rather than too heavy dumbbells.

### Music.

Old-fashioned waltzes like the "Boston Dip" are best for these exercises. Scotch airs, and airs from popular operas in this time can easily be adapted by a skilful musician. For the Anvil Chorus the air from the opera of "Il Trovatore" called "Anvil Chorus" is used.

# PERCUSSION.

This exercise has special value for those who are not vigorous, and for all at the close of a lesson, as it aids greatly in giving a general glow to the system, and will prevent lameness afterward. What timid beginners fear to be actual injury is often nothing but muscular soreness, which may be wholly removed by a little brisk percussion, or rubbing the parts affected with a coarse towel or a brush.

I do not give this exercise, however, any prominence for use in large classes, as it is almost impossible, from the nature of the exercise, to preserve order or regularity. The sound of so many hands drowns not only the teacher's voice but the music itself.

## Percussion.

The following order suggests what may be used with profit by moderate-sized classes, and by single individuals:—

Position: Couples stand facing the same way, the one in front bending slightly forward with arms folded for the first exercise, keeping perfectly erect in all the others. Partner stands ready to begin on first beat of the music.

No. 1. Percuss the shoulders quickly, then reverse the position and repeat.

No. 2. Percuss the small of the back. Reverse, and repeat.

No. 3. Percuss right side, under uplifted arm. Reverse, and repeat.

No. 4. Percuss left side. Reverse, and repeat.

No. 5. Percuss both sides. Reverse, and repeat.

No. 6. Percuss extended right arm, which is constantly turned from right to left. Reverse, and repeat.

No. 7. Percuss extended left arm. Reverse, and repeat.

No. 8.  Percuss both arms.  Reverse, and repeat.

No. 9.  Percuss chest, not too vigorously.  Reverse, and repeat.

### Cautions.

Avoid changing position in the line, and keep perfect time.  Percuss gently at first, and always alternating the blows; viz., one hand, the left, following the right.  Never use the hands simultaneously.

Music: Jigs must always be used, but played only moderately fast.

# MUTUAL HELP EXERCISES.

These, like percussion, are not particularly desirable for large classes, but are valuable as affording complete change, and they can also be performed without the aid of music.

Position: The class by threes all stand facing the teacher, with heels together and hands down at sides.

No. 1. The one in middle steps forward, with arms down at sides, hands firmly closed, and draws them slowly up to armpits, while those at sides with hands on wrist and shoulders resist forcibly.

No. 2. Middle one steps back, arms extended in front, draws them back to chest, then thrust them out again, the others resisting as before.

No. 3. Middle one forward, arms thrust up, bring slowly back to shoulders, and thrust up again, others resisting.

No. 4. Middle one forward, arms thrust out at sides, bend forearm while others resist.

No. 5. Middle one forward, arms extended in front, carry back to horizontal at sides, while others resist.

No. 6. Middle one forward, arms thrust up, then carry to position in front; others resist.

No. 7. Middle one forward, arms down at sides, those on right and left clasp hands back of middle one's neck, who is slowly lowered without bending the knees.

No. 8. Middle one forward, arms down at sides, those on right and left seize hand and wrist of middle one, who slowly arches body forward and back.

No. 9. Middle one forward, arms down at sides, those at right and left seize hands and armpit while middle one sits down, then change hands to top of shoulder while middle one slowly rises, resisting as before.

No. 10. Middle one bend forward, arms folded, while the others percuss shoulders and back.

No. 11. Middle one forward while the others percuss both arms, which are constantly turned. Let those on right and left in turn, change with middle one, and repeat the above exercises.

## Caution.

Stand firmly, and be careful not to let the hands slip, as there is danger of the middle one's falling in exercise No. 7. The only music required is signals, like those used at the beginning of the wand exercises.

# BEAN-BAGS.

These bags are made of stout bed-ticking, about ten inches square, and two-thirds filled with beans. They should always be kept away from the dust as much as possible.

If these exercises are to be performed by couples, partners should stand facing each other, about six feet apart. Throw the bag to partner from chest with both hands, from chest with right hand, then with left. From behind the head with both hands, then with right and left. Bag behind the back, throw with both hands, with right, with left. Stand back to back, throw bag over head with both hands, with right, with left. Take two bags, throw them with right and catch them with left. Throw them with left and catch them with right. Throw them with both and catch them with both hands.

Same exercises can be taken with three or more bags as the skill increases.

Vary the exercises by taking them in quartettes, standing a greater distance apart. Stand again in two rows down the hall, six feet apart and facing each other. Starting at the head with a bag in each leader's hand, let it be thrown to every other one till all have caught it, when it must be returned in same manner.

The leader getting bag first on return trip should hold up bag as signal of victory. Stand in same rows, but face up the hall, then pass bag over head to next one in line, and so on to the last, and back the same way. Any number of bags can be used in this manner.

# MARCHING.

This is the most fascinating form of all gymnastic work; and with bright, interested leaders, an almost endless variety of exercises can be improvised beyond those I shall here describe. I can safely say that I alone have added a hundred changes to the first simple exercises, which I practised at school.

As many as practicable will be given, but some are so intricate as to defy description, and can only be appreciated by being seen.

Dancing steps of all kinds, and figures from quadrilles and the German can be introduced with beautiful effect.

### Position in Marching.

In single file marches, hands should be placed on the hips, with thumbs turned back, head, shoulders and hips well back, chin down, and feet turned slightly out. In order to cultivate an erect and graceful carriage in walking, as well as in marching, too much attention cannot be paid to these directions. Throw the foot outward, and always rest first upon the toes more than on other parts of the foot. Those who are inclined to turn one, or both feet in, can often overcome this habit by taking great pains during the gymnastic march. Never drag the feet, nor carry the hips forward, and always keep perfect time with the music. Good leaders should only be allowed to assist, as apart from the music, the success of the march depends upon their skill, self-possession, and above all, ability to keep those of the class wanting in time, in perfect step with the music. The position of the one at the rear is nearly as important as the leader; for upon her devolves also the duty of keeping the class in good order, and allowing no laggards to fall out of step or line.

Some of the principal steps require a description at first, as they are the foundation of all the figures used in marching.

*Leaping* is running, only the steps are shorter, the knees more bent, and the weight thrown chiefly upon the toes.

*Skipping* is sliding one foot before the other, the leading foot pointing in the direction about to be taken, and the other foot nearly at right angles with it.

*The short side step* consists of hopping twice upon the left foot carried diagonally to the left, then twice upon the right, out at right side.

*The long side step.* This is more difficult, and the left foot leads as before, but closely followed by the right foot just behind it; then hop twice on the left. Now carry the right foot to the right, left behind it, then hop twice on the right. Rather long steps, almost, at the side are necessary.

*Short front step.* This is like the short side step, only hopping twice on left, then

## Marching. 57

twice on right, just in front instead of at the side. The waltz step, heel and toe polka, the racquet, the Evangeline quickstep, two or three twisted steps, which cannot here be described, must all be taken if in the double march in one way. Hands may be crossed in front, or they may rest upon the shoulders of partners or neighbors; but the leaping step must always be performed with hands closely clasped and lifted high.

*In pushing,* partners clasp hands, step four feet apart, and with unoccupied hand on hip push steadily, and march slowly in line to the foot of the hall.

*Pulling* differs only in starting with feet near together, hands tightly clasped, and pulling with full and equal strength down the hall. In all other double exercises it is right to have partners separate in front of platform, and each leader turning square corners, lead each line in single-file order up the side to upper centre, where partners again join. But in pushing and pulling, the one marching on left crosses before her partner so as to take, at the other end of hall, the same exercise with the other hand. The easiest of all marches comes first, for a description.

## The Single File March.

As the name indicates, all the following changes are to be performed by the class, led by the teacher, or some competent leader, in single file order.

First, march up, down, and across the hall with shoulders and hips thrown back, and hands on hips. This position of the hands is to give uniformity in appearance, and to aid in expanding the chest, and should be carefully avoided except while marching. Take two or three turns about the hall to enable all to get into good position in the line, about two feet apart, and also in step with the music. Cross the hall from side to side, six or eight times, beginning at upper end of hall and ending close by platform. Cross the hall diagonally; repeat on the other side. Turn, and march down the centre, rising on tips of toes; again down centre on the heels; again half way down on right heel and left toe; the other half on left toe and right heel. March up right side of hall with body inclined to right, for half a dozen steps; change to the left for the same time. March, bending the body forward, then bend it back. March down centre without bending knees; again bending knees, and keeping the body perfectly erect. Take the centre of hall again, and march half way down, bending to right, with left hand behind the head, the rest of the way reverse the position. Now march with toes turned out as far as possible, change, and turn the toes in. Exaggerate these exercises, as they employ unused muscles very advantageously.

Form large circle by joining hands; all skip to right, then to left: march to right, then to left; leap to right, then to left. All stand, then rise upon the toes at first beat of music, and sit down on the heels on the second. Vary this exercise, if the class is a large one, by forming four circles, one within the other, one leader standing alone in centre. Then repeat the rising and sitting exercises just performed in large circles, only every other circle rise while the other sits. Every other circle skip, while the others leap; then half march one way while half leap the other; or one half leap, while the other skips. All, while in this position, stand still for a moment, then stamp alternately left and right feet with the music, and march evenly to centre. Stamp again, and all retreat evenly until extended in former position in the circles. Lift hands high, and all leap to the centre, then all march softly to centre, and back to place. Break the circles, and with leader at head form again in single file, and march half way round the hall with arms clasped behind the back, then behind the head the other half of distance. Change to the centre of hall, leap down in single file, of course, and again with longer steps. Again with short or long side step. The heel and toe polka, waltz step, and other dancing steps can be at any time introduced, always remembering to put an easy step or exercise between the difficult ones.

Wind the class up in what is called a "Labyrinth," which is marching in slowly diminishing circles till the leader reaches the centre, when she makes a short turn, retracing her steps, closely followed by the whole class. Each person must keep two feet from the one in front, and avoid contact with any.

Another pretty change is to cross the upper end of hall, marching. turn, cross, leaping, next march, next skip, next march, and so on until the foot of the hall is reached. March for a short time down the hall with both hands on shoulders of one in front. Repeat, taking leaping. short and long side steps. The latter step is particularly pretty, taken in this way. While the hands are still resting on shoulders various turns and curves about the hall may be taken, with quite remarkable effect; and a capital exercise, while hands are in same position, is to keep very close together, and march after the style of convicts in the prison-yards. This will do more to give an idea of step and time than any other exercise. Vary, by taking a long step diagonally to right, another to left, keeping perfect step and time with the music.

### Regular or Double March.

For this march partners should be chosen with regard to equal size and strength; and in forming pains should be taken to place the tallest and strongest at the head.

It is well to begin by marching arm in arm once around the hall; then stopping for a moment at the upper end, join hands and begin with any of the simpler exercises, such as skipping slowly down the centre, separating, and marching up the sides in single-file order, where partners again meet.

Take in turn leaping, pushing with both left and right hands, leaping with longer steps, pulling with both left and right hands; then the side steps, both short and long, and two or three of the dancing steps that are now understood by nearly all young ladies in school. Many easy changes with the skipping step can be introduced between the more difficult exercises; as for instance, skipping down the hall face to face with partner, four feet apart; again, and clap hands in time with the music; again, skipping four steps face to face with partner, then reversing four steps, and so on to the end of the hall. Skip down the hall shoulder to shoulder with partner; skip with the hands in front lowered, the other hands lifted.

Still another way: start shoulder to shoulder, skip diagonally to the right four steps, then to the left four steps, meeting partner. or skip in different directions at the same time four steps and turn, then skipping four steps toward partner, joining on the fifth.

After leaving partner at foot of the hall, always turn square corners, and keep the line on the side in perfect order. The diagonal figure is formed by stopping at the upper corner of hall, then marching to the centre, where partners touch shoulders, separate, and again march diagonally to opposite corners. This may be repeated, and instead of touching shoulders on meeting, each one passes in front of her partner, and marches on as before. This is a figure that can be made even more attractive by being performed by couples instead of singly.

March down centre of hall, and at the foot both leaders turn to the right, the next couple to the left, and so on, every other couple following the leaders to the right. Meet at the head of hall, and march down four abreast, keeping perfect step and time, and a straight line must always be preserved. Next time leap four abreast, with hands lifted, and head and shoulders well back. Again, skip by fours, joining the two hands in front down low, and the other hands very high. March with hands clasped and arms extended at full length. This is a very simple but effective exercise, and a restful one.

Next, take the side step by fours, and in this exercise better support can be given by placing hands on shoulders. The long side step should also be taken this way, and taken alternately by fours, the first four leading to the right.

It is well, while taking steps four and eight abreast, to reverse at foot of the hall, and march back, reverse again at the head of hall.

Other exercises that can be taken by couples, are the following: Leap backward, march backward, lifting clasped hands very high, and taking care not to step on the feet of those before. Join right hands. one skip while the other leaps.

March at arm's length. march with hands lifted high, then return under the uplifted arms, or turn and march up the hall close behind the line, and leap down the centre. When marching four abreast a pretty figure is formed by wheeling by twos at the foot of the hall, marching up close behind the line to the upper end, where all turn face to face, and at the same time face across the hall, about four feet apart. All join hands, stamp, and march to the centre, where four from the head of inner line join hands, and skip by twos down between the lines. Meanwhile all stamp and approach again, and four more go down the centre. Repeat till all from inside are back in position just behind their partners. Repeat, stamping and approaching four steps, while the other line skips down the centre by twos. Lead off from the top by twos, and march slowly round the hall to rest.

The old dance called Sicilian circle, can be introduced for sake of variety, and the order is as follows. While marching, every other couple face in the opposite direction.

 1st. Four hands round, turn quite to place
 2d. Ladies' chain.
 3d. Right and left.

4th. All four cross hands in the centre, swing half way round, and back to place.

5th. Forward and back, forward and back again, pass through, meeting the next couple. Swing four hands round, and so on, repeating till the leaders have made the circuit of the hall.

A difficult, but beautiful figure, consists of the gradual and perfect changing from single file on the side to four, eight, and sixteen abreast. Then reverse, thus bringing the class back into single file order. This requires skilful leaders, and much practice to bring about a satisfactory result.

While marching four, eight, and sixteen abreast, the hands should be dropped at the sides, shoulder against shoulder, keeping close to next neighbor.

Another very pretty figure is to form a hollow square, in the following manner: —

Let the class form eight abreast at head of the hall, and march slowly down once, keeping the lines six or eight feet apart; separate, and wheel by fours at the foot of the hall; march still more slowly from the head until half way down the centre. The first line of eight stand still, only marking time with the left foot, while the second line wheels to the right, the third line to left, and the fourth closes up, making the square complete. If there are more than the thirty-two comprising the square, in the class, move this square lower down the hall, and form one or more above it.

While marching eight abreast, instead of separating by fours at the foot of the hall, a pretty change is effected by having the class all face to the right and march off, one line at a time, single file, until all are in line on the the side of the hall. Another way is to swing the first line to the right, the second to the left, and so on, till all are at the sides.

The lines must be kept perfectly straight while wheeling to right or left. The one at end of line in centre remains almost stationary, while the one at the opposite end moves quite rapidly. Always remember, in this and in all other large figures to face a little to the left, keeping close to the next neighbor.

When classes do not number over thirty, it is best to keep them all in one company, but for a much larger number it is easier and prettier to divide the class equally. Place good leaders at the head of each division, and keep the two lines about eight feet apart, leading from the head of the hall, as in ordinary marching. Part of the time let both companies take exactly the same exercises at the same time; then change, and give the leaders an opportunity to see how many different changes they can recall, and originate. Never allow one leader to use the same exercise that the other is taking at the same time.

The wheel is one of the handsomest of the large figures, and not at all difficult.

Move the class very slowly, four abreast, nearly down the hall. Let all those who are at the end of lines on the right keep almost immovable, while the rest march slowly about the hall. Each line forms a spoke in the wheel, and those at the "hub" must join hands or touch shoulders in order to keep well together. After turning twice round the hall, the leader at the end of first line marches slowly up the side of hall, followed by end one from each line. In the mean time the wheel continues to turn, and on the second revolution, all again from the ends, follow the second leader. So continue till the class is in four long lines, one within the other, and marching very slowly. All pay strict attention to the leaders, who soon form four abreast, and followed in same way by the whole class, march quite round the hall. This is a good time for singing, which is one very important and pleasing feature of the Gymnasium. Clasp hands behind the back, or extend the arms, resting hands upon neighbors' shoulders, and sing with all the spirit and strength possible.

Sing once during every march, and let it be a time for slow, restful figures, or for the last two or three turns about the hall before the class is dismissed. When the class is large several more difficult figures can be formed.

One of these is called the pyramid: While marching single file, the leader rests half way down centre of hall, two stand behind her, three next, four next, and so on, till all the class are in position. Face to the right, leader march off first, followed by each line in turn till all are again in single-file order. Always repeat this.

Another is called the double cross, and is formed in this manner:—

From the head of the hall while marching four abreast, four lead down centre single file. The next four wheel to right, next four to left, joining eight abreast behind the first four. Then four more lead single file, four wheel to right, four to left, and so on. If the class is very large eight should lead, followed by sixteen. While marching down the centre sixteen abreast, it is very good practice to separate, wheel eight each way, again separate on the side, march four abreast, separate, march two abreast, and from head of hall march in single-file order down centre.

To cultivate attention and promptness of action, when starting with partners, march a few steps, reverse, each dropping the arm, and turning toward partners, march on a few steps in opposite direction, skip a few steps, reverse quickly and march. Reverse again, and leap; reverse, and skip; reverse, and march single file. Change quickly back to partners, then to single file again, to four, eight, and sixteen abreast; then back to single file or partners again. March with partner from head of hall very slowly. After a few steps the next couple separate, right one stepping to right of leader, left to left of other leader. Third and fourth couples separate a little later, each, and join in the same manner. Then the leaders from the next eight step forward, next couple separate, and so on, till the class is marching eight abreast down the hall. All wheel to right, and march down centre with hands crossed behind the back. Always repeat this.

### RING MARCH.

Choose partners, and each one carry a ring in the right hand. Select such exercises as have already been described that can well be performed with rings. Join rings at upper end of hall and pull once. return and pull with other hand. Push with right and left, then with both hands.

Join hands four abreast, and take leaping, skipping, and all the side and front steps. Cross hands, with rings in front, and take the waltz, heel-and-toe polka, or any of the before-mentioned dancing steps. Take them in couples, or four, eight and sixteen abreast. Join rings, and march down the hall with rings and hands extended; reverse, and leap back with hands uplifted.

All the exercises given for the single-file march, particularly in circles, are more effective when performed with the rings. What is called the basket figure in quadrilles, can be well introduced; and an extremely pretty figure is formed by joining rings throughout the class, keeping in single-file order, and wind up in the labyrinth, or carry the line in serpentine curves about the hall. Another change may be introduced in this way: Form a line on each side of the hall, leaders standing just at the upper end. Join the rings, raise them high and leap to the centre. When the two lines are exactly face to face, drop hands to position on the hips; all face quickly down the hall and march single file till the lines are again in position. Cross the hands with rings in front while standing in same position, and march carefully till both lines meet; then face down the hall and march round to upper centre, join partners, and drop rings at sides. Form two large circles; while all in one circle lift the hands and rings high, the leader of the other breaks her circle, and passing under the uplifted hands of those nearest her, leads her company in and out between every other couple till she brings her circle back to place, with hands uplifted. The other leader repeats this exercise.

## Wand March.

The wand is held in right hand resting against right shoulder, left hand always down at side instead of on the hip. The music, as a rule, should be slow, and regular march time is better than the quicker music used for the fancy steps and dancing figures of the marches. Of course many of the changes already given can well be introduced here; but there are many others peculiarly adapted to this style of marching, and effort should be made to make it as unlike the ring, single file and double marches as possible. March slowly round the room by twos; reverse, march by fours; reverse, by eights; reverse, back to fours, back to two abreast, still marching round the room and not down the centre. Partners march side by side with wands behind the shoulders, behind the head. Join the hands in front, leap down the centre with hands in that position. Down the centre again with longer leaping steps, and with hands and wands uplifted.

Skip with wands joined between partners, and pointing up and down the hall. March down centre two feet apart with wands lifted high over head. Meet again at head of hall, step four feet from partner. touch ends of wands high over head. The next couple pass under them, taking same position just beside the first couple. All follow till a long bridge is formed, under which the class follows the leader. Another somewhat similar exercise is formed by marching slowly down the hall with wands joined and lifted as high as possible. and at the foot of the hall turning and passing under the wands of the whole class. Partners separate at foot of hall, march in single file up the sides, stop at upper corner, all face across the hall.

Mark time with left foot. face the left, and

at the word of command from the leader all march (starting with left foot always) to the centre of hall. On reaching partners, face down the hall, and march down and separate as usual.

Another way, upon meeting in the centre face to face, is for each to pass to left of partner, and cross the hall, keeping the line as straight as possible. Reverse, and repeat the order, marching across the hall, and the diagonal changes have a pretty effect with the uplifted wands.

Pass into single-file order, partners resting their wands on each other's shoulders. Lift, and return the wands to that position twice. Drop wands down at sides, raise to perpendicular twice, then from shoulder at side, and to horizontal at side twice.

Again from overhead down to shoulder twice. Zigzag across the hall, wind up in the labyrinth, form a circle, and then all face to the centre, and charge with wands. first right, then left, as in the regular wand exercise.

All march to centre of circle stamping, return softly to place. All face out, and charge as before, left, then right, pointing the wands diagonally forward each time.

March single file half-way up the hall, on each side.

Turn square corner, and four from each line march to centre of hall, where they remain standing face to face.

Four more pass in behind them, and so continue till all are standing in the same position. The leader, giving a signal, marches with partner out and down the hall, followed by class, two by two; each in turning must march into the leader's place before starting down the hall. The wheel formed while marching with wands has a good effect, and only one difference must be observed: the hands must be dropped down at sides instead of joining one with next neighbor.

### Cautions.

Never march too long.

Never march when tired. Pupils are very

apt to think that as marching is more enjoyable than other exercises it can be taken when too tired to do anything else.

While marching with rings the utmost pains should be taken not to move swiftly when they are joined, as in circles; and while the wands are used there is some danger of hitting those behind with the wand while changing its position at foot of the hall.

# CHAPTER ON DRESS.

Much thought and consideration have been bestowed upon the preparation of a suitable gymnastic dress, which should combine all that is most needful for a warm, properly fitting, and withal, cheap garment. In addition to the careful examination of different styles of dress, as worn in the classes of Dr. Lewis, and many others, I have had the personal supervision of all the gymnastic suits made for the students of Smith College, for the past six years. I feel justified, therefore in saying, as the result of such experience, that I have at last a model, which if always properly made, is very nearly perfect. This dress is so simple that with the following carefully prepared directions and measurements, it can be easily made at home. The best material is coarse, but not thin, twilled flannel. This hangs and wears better than any lighter, handsomer goods. A sufficiently good quality can be purchased at wholesale from thirty to thirty-five cents per yard; at retail from thirty-five to forty cents. All things considered, dark blue is the color to choose, provided you can get a shade that will not crock badly. All blue and some other colors are more or less uncertain, but there is a great difference in this respect. Take a sample and test, by rubbing vigorously on white cloth. A thin lining cambric can be used to advantage on this account for the waist and sleeves only. It is desirable for no other reason, as the dress is sufficiently warm without it. Suits of this material of ordinary width require from seven and a quarter to eight and a half yards, according to size of wearer. With the first named amount for a person of medium size, the flannel drawers, which always accompany this dress, must be pieced at top with cambric, and many prefer this way, while with eight and a half yards for a person of the same size, there will be material sufficient to make the drawers entirely of flannel. These drawers are essential for warmth, and are much less conspicuous than those ordinarily worn, which these of course entirely cover. They should be long enough to reach a little below the knee, where they are confined by elastic cord, and show very little, if any below the dress. The skirt should be trimmed with a plaited flounce five or six inches deep after it is finished; placed not on the skirt, but at the lower edge, as seen in frontispiece. This flounce should be stitched on a little below its upper edge, to afford a heading. Several rows of white, red or old gold braid above the flounce add to the effect, and the same trimmings of course on the waist, collar, cuffs, belt and pocket-laps, with buttons to match.

The whole cost of such a dress is six dollars and twenty-five cents. Deduct from this two dollars and a half, the usual price of those who make up such dresses by the quantity, and the expense of one gotten up wholly at home would be three dollars and seventy-five cents. This is when the goods are bought at wholesale price. The great mistake is often made of overtrimming, thus adding to the cost and weight of a dress whose leading characteristics should be durability and simplicity. It is far more economical to have classes wear a uniform. The suits are then cut to much better advantage, while the class will make a finer appearance as a whole, than if individual taste was allowed. Everything depends upon the cutting and fitting of such dresses. The skirt has one plain breadth in the back, one slightly gored in the front, and a gore on each side. The length of the skirt after the flounce is on should invariably be seven inches from the floor at the back, and eight inches in front. A longer skirt is difficult to manage, and a shorter one awkward and unnecessary. Width of skirt two and one-fourth yards. The waist is quite loose, and long enough under the arms to enable the wearer to thrust the arms directly up without drawing upon the waist belt at all. There should be plenty of room across the chest, and the shoulder seam measures just six inches in length. After the sleeve is in, a small plait just above the top of the sleeve is made, reducing the length of the shoulder seam to exactly five inches. This gives all the breadth required, and the plait enables the wearer to lift the arm without restraint, and greatly improves the appearance of the figure. The sleeve is what is commonly known as a shirt sleeve, being perfectly straight, and having the inside seam slightly shorter at top and bottom than the outside. It is prettiest when finished with a deep turned-over cuff, trimmed with braid, and three or four buttons up the back. A sailor or any large collar is used. If the belts are trimmed with braid, or to match the rest of the dress, there is no necessity for outside belts, as the skirts are sewn firmly to the waist, and a pocket inserted in the old-fashioned way in the right side seam, with cover or lap trimmed with braid and buttons. Bands of soft woollen in gold, crimson or white can be substituted for the braid, which is, however, the simplest and cheapest form of ornamentation. A short white or flannel skirt must be worn always, and stockings of dark blue, cardinal, or black are in the best taste. While strapped slippers or low shoes can be worn with propriety, an easy broad-soled, low-heeled buttoned boot is by far the best. The old-fashioned low slipper offers no support to the ankles, which are often, in consequence, liable to sprains during the marching and dumb-bell exercises. High heels and corsets are the two great evils to be avoided, and it seems utterly absurd that any sensible girl should need a word of caution in regard to what is so obvious a drawback to all movements in the direction of health.

whether it be exercise in the Gymnasium, or out of doors. A thick, well-fitting, but loose under-waist should take the place of all forms of corsets, and the shoe which is destined to be habitually worn in the Gymnasium is low, broad, made of soft serge, tied over the instep, and with very low heel. In these all difficult steps can be taken with ease, and walking and running can be performed as naturally as by boys. How many can boast of having seen a young lady of the period run with ease and grace? and not one in twenty of our school girls walks with erect and graceful carriage. Tight dresses, heavy skirts and high-heeled boots can certainly be all done away with in the Gymnasium, and this movement in the right direction ought to lead to reform in all home and street dress.

One word more of caution in regard to dress after exercising. If necessary to go at once into the outside air, a cloak or long dress skirt and wrap of some sort should be put on over the short dress, while in winter overshoes, or some other protection for both feet and ankles, must be added. Simple as are these precautions, many will fail to use them unless repeatedly urged to do so; and the colds that often follow such unnecessary exposure only serve to convince those not favorably disposed to these exercises of their dangerous character.

# GYMNASTIC MUSIC.

As soon as a good musician becomes acquainted with the exact time required for the different exercises, almost any air can be adapted for each and every one of them.

At first, however, it is necessary to have some special music that can be easily procured at any music store.

The following list contains only such selections as have been thoroughly tested in the College Gymnasium: —

### Free Gymnastics.

"Northern Route," Galop, by Charles Smith.
Chorus, "Good Night," from Evangeline.
March, from Boccacio.
"Just Once More," Galop.

"Jolly Brothers," Galop.
"Triton," March.
"Pizzacata," Polka, by Strauss.

### Wands.

"Haymaker's," Schottische, by W. A. Briggs. This is the only music that can be fully recommended for the Wands.

### Rings.

"Blue Danube" Waltzes, by Strauss.
"Artist's Life," Waltz, by Strauss.
Selections from "La Mascotte."

*For the Quartette Exercises, with Rings:*
"High Life is Splendid,"
"Saratoga Waltzes," by Bowles.

### Dumb-Bells.

"Academic" Waltzes, by Strauss,
"Autograph" Waltzes, by Strauss.
"Thousand-and-one Nights," by Strauss.
Waltz, Lanciers, by Dodworth.

"Boston Dip," Waltz.

"Annie Laurie," and other Scotch airs

*For the Anvil Chorus:*

Anvil Chorus, from Il Trovatore.

### Marches.

"Triton," March, by Bowles.

Racquet Galop, by Kate Simmons.

"Queen's," Polka, by Raff.

"Switzer Boy," College Song.

Vocal Lanciers.

Virginia Reel.

"Life let us Cherish."

Secret Love.

The Caledonians.

Turtle Dove Polka.

"Queen's," Polka.

"Puck."

Heel and Toe, from "Fatinitza."

"Northern Route," Galop.

"Soldier's Joy," College Song.

"Life let us Cherish."

March, from "The Pirates."
The "Pirate's Serenade."
March, from "Faust."

---

# INDIAN CLUBS.

MANY of the club exercises, as given in our regular gymnasiums, are exceedingly difficult, and are not practicable in class drill for young ladies and children. For this reason, there will here be introduced a few only of the more simple exercises, such as can be used with music.

The size of the club should always be the first thing considered: eighteen inches long, and three inches thick, for young ladies; fifteen inches long, and two inches thick, for children.

The club exercises, in some respects, differ widely from all others.

They are chiefly useful in cultivating endurance: they bring into play and greatly strengthen the muscles of the neck and shoulders. They also aid greatly in overcoming the habit of stooping.

These movements should always be taken more slowly than other exercises, and the times of rest should be more frequent.

Great effort must be made to secure a straight line in the arm and club, both for appearance' sake, and to get the full value of the exercise. It will be found more difficult to obtain accuracy with the clubs than with dumb-bells, wands, or rings.

### Exercises.

No. 1. Clubs held firmly down at the sides. Carry the right arm, without bending the elbow, up to the horizontal in front, then back to first position. The left arm performs the same. Then both arms together, twice.

This fills a strain of music, as all the movements are made on accented beats only.

No. 2. On the last unaccented beat of the last strain, bring both arms into the horizontal position in front. Starting with them in that position carry the right arm from the horizontal in front, to the perpendicular over the shoulder, and back again to the horizontal, once. Left arm, the same. Both arms together, twice. This completes the strain.

No. 3. Let the clubs fall on the last unaccented beat into first position, down at sides. Now bring the right club from this position to the perpendicular over the shoulder, and back again, once. Left club, the same. Both clubs together, twice.

No. 4. Starting in the first position, carry the right club to the horizontal, directly at the side, and back, once. The left club, the same. Both together, twice.

No. 5. On last unaccented beat of last strain carry both clubs into the horizontal at the side. Now raise the right club and arm into the perpendicular over the shoulder, and return to the horizontal, once. Left club, the same. Both clubs together, twice.

No. 6. On the last unaccented beat of the last strain, drop the clubs to first position down at sides. Now carry the right club through the side sweep to the perpendicular, over the shoulder, and return to first position. Left club, the same. Both clubs together, twice.

No. 7. Starting in first position, raise the right club to the horizontal in front, and, at the same time, raise the left club to the horizontal at the side. Now bring them both back to first position. On the third beat, carry the right club up to the horizontal at the side; and the left club to the horizontal in front. Back to first position. Repeat these two movements, which will complete the strain.

No. 8. On the last unaccented beat of last strain, bring both clubs into the following position: the right club horizontal in front, the left club horizontal at side. Carry the clubs to the perpendicular over the shoulders, then bring them down to the horizontal again, but let the right club fall into the last position of left, and the left club into position of right. In order to complete the strain of music, repeat the whole of this exercise.

No. 9. Lift the right club to the perpendicular over the shoulder, left club to the horizontal in front, change position evenly, throughout the strain.

No. 10. Lift both clubs to the perpendicular, over the shoulders, bringing them both down to the horizontal in front, and on the next beat carry them slowly in same line to the horizontal at the sides. On the next beat carry the clubs up to the perpendicular over the shoulders; on the next beat, to the horizontal in front; on the next beat, again to the horizontal at the side; on the next beat, again to the perpendicular over the shoulders; on the next beat, to the horizontal in front; on the next beat, to the perpendicular over the shoulders.

No. 11. On the last unaccented beat of the last strain bring the clubs into the horizontal position in front. Holding the arms firmly in this position, without bending the elbows, carry the right club, by a slow turn of the wrist, over upon the right arm, letting it strike the wrist and arm; then on the next accented beat carry it back again to the extended horizontal position in front. The left arm performs the same. Both together, twice.

No. 12. On the last unaccented beat of last strain, carry the arms around to the horizontal at the sides, holding the arms firmly in that position; by a slow turn of the wrist carry the right club over upon the right arm, as in last exercise; then on next beat carry it back again to the extended horizontal position in front. Left club the same. Both together, twice.

No. 13. At the close of last exercise bring the clubs back again to the horizontal in front, and holding both arms firmly in this position lift both clubs to the perpendicular: all of this must be done on the last unaccented beat of last strain. Now on the first beat let the right club fall directly outward at right angles with the arm, down to the horizontal, and then bring it back to the perpendicular. Left club, the same. Both clubs together, twice.

No. 14. Extending the arms to the horizontal in front, the clubs perpendicular; let the right club fall down to the horizontal at right angles with the right arm, and towards the other hand. Carry it back again to the perpendicular. Left club, the same. Both clubs together, twice.

No. 15. On the last unaccented beat of last strain, bring the arms around to the horizontal at the sides, the clubs being held in the perpendicular attitude. Now let the right club fall down into position of hanging behind. Keep the arms exactly horizontal, and bring the clubs back again to the perpendicular at sides. Left club, the same. Both clubs together, twice.

No. 16. Holding the arms horizontal at the sides, with the clubs perpendicular, repeat the last exercise, except that the clubs must fall down in front instead of behind.

www.ingramcontent.com/pod-product-compliance
Lightning Source LLC
Chambersburg PA
CBHW020859160426
43192CB00007B/986